I Can Be Anything!

I CAN BE A CHEF

By Miller Slenzak

Please visit our website, www.garethstevens.com. For a free color catalog of all our high-quality books, call toll free 1-800-542-2595 or fax 1-877-542-2596.

Library of Congress Cataloging-in-Publication Data

Names: Slenzak, Miller, author.
Title: I can be a chef / Miller Slenzak.
Description: New York : Gareth Stevens Publishing, [2019] | Series: I can be anything! | Includes index.
Identifiers: LCCN 2017045286| ISBN 9781538217535 (library bound) | ISBN 9781538217580 (pbk.) | ISBN 9781538217597 (6 pack)
Subjects: LCSH: Cooking–Vocational guidance–Juvenile literature.
Classification: LCC TX652.4 .S545 2019 | DDC 641.5023–dc23
LC record available at https://lccn.loc.gov/2017045286

First Edition

Published in 2019 by
Gareth Stevens Publishing
111 East 14th Street, Suite 349
New York, NY 10003

Editor: Kate Mikoley
Designer: Laura Bowen

Photo credits: Cover, p. 1 (kid) Andy-pix/Shutterstock.com; cover, p.1 (background) Tyler Olson/Shutterstock.com; pp. 5, 11, 23 wavebreakmedia/Shutterstock.com; p. 7 Roman Kosolapov/Shutterstock.com; p. 9 Gorodenkoff/Shutterstock.com; pp. 13, 24 Kondor83/Shutterstock.com; pp. 15, 24 otnaydur/Shutterstock.com; p. 17 Rawpixel.com/Shutterstock.com; pp. 19, 24 OkFoto/Shutterstock.com; p. 21 Evgeny Litvinov/Shutterstock.com.

Printed in the United States of America

CPSIA compliance information: Batch #CS18GS: For further information contact Gareth Stevens, New York, New York at 1-800-542-2595.

Contents

Chefs cook yummy food!

They work in restaurants.
These are places
where people eat.

They work in a kitchen. This is where food is made.

Some wear big hats.

They use pots and pans.

They also use an oven.

They make the menu.
This is the list of food.

Menu
Starter
Goat Cheese Salad
Tuscan Garden Salad
Main
Salmon with Lemon and Butter Sauce
Baby Rack of Lamb
with Fresh Herbs and Spices
Dessert
White Chocolate Cheesecake
Passion Fruit Cake
Grille
Homemade

My aunt is a chef.
She makes pasta.

Some chefs make cake.

I can be a chef.
So can you!

Words to Know

oven pasta pot

Index